STAGECOACH IN THE TWENTY-FIRST CENTURY

KEITH A. JENKINSON

AMBERLEY

First published 2019

Amberley Publishing
The Hill, Stroud
Gloucestershire, GL5 4EP

www.amberley-books.com

Copyright © Keith A. Jenkinson, 2019

The right of Keith A. Jenkinson to be identified
as the Author of this work has been asserted
in accordance with the Copyright, Designs and
Patents Act 1988.

ISBN 978 1 4456 7879 5 (print)
ISBN 978 1 4456 7880 1 (ebook)

All rights reserved. No part of this book may be
reprinted or reproduced or utilised in any form
or by any electronic, mechanical or other means,
now known or hereafter invented, including
photocopying and recording, or in any information
storage or retrieval system, without the permission
in writing from the Publishers.

British Library Cataloguing in Publication Data.
A catalogue record for this book is available from
the British Library.

Origination by Amberley Publishing.
Printed in the UK.

Introduction

Born in 1980, during the remaining years of the twentieth century Stagecoach had built itself into a massive global company through its purchase of numerous bus operators throughout the UK and across five continents. As it moved into the new millennium, its desire for further expansion showed no signs of stagnation, and although it disposed of a number of operations, it countered these with the acquisition of others, as can be seen from the following account.

After a quiet start, in April 2000 Stagecoach sold its Porterbrook railway rolling stock-leasing company to Abbey National before embarking once again on the acquisition trail during the same month when Stagecoach Fife purchased Allison's, Dunfermline, together with its fleet of thirty elderly double-deckers. Also during April, Stagecoach purchased some of the services of Greater Manchester's independent Universal Buses Ltd of Chadderton, which was an offshoot of Bu Val Buses of Littleborough. Following this, in May Stagecoach Bluebird acquired the business and thirteen vehicles of JW Coaches, Banchory, which it maintained as a separate company, retaining its livery. Still seeking expansion, in June Stagecoach Cumberland bought Heysham Travel, along with thirty buses and coaches from Arriva North West, thus strengthening its position in Morecambe and Lancaster. Meanwhile, in a bid to eliminate competition in south-east Wales, in September it purchased part of the business of Pontypool-based independent bus operator Phil Anslow Travel together with twenty-eight minibuses through its Red & White subsidiary. Then, as the year was drawing to a close, in November Stagecoach introduced a new corporate livery, fleet name style and logo, which replaced its familiar stripes with a softer colour scheme, although this retained its red, orange and blue colours. This began to be steadily rolled out across the UK as vehicles were repainted. Earlier in the year, Stagecoach had repatriated a number of air-conditioned Plaxton-bodied Dennis Dart SLFs from Hong King Citybus and put the first of these in service in Devon.

After taking stock of its operations in the UK and overseas, Stagecoach took the decision to dispose of its underperforming operations in East Lancashire, and to this end sold its Ribble depots at Clitheroe, Blackburn and Bolton, together with its Burnley & Pendle subsidiary, to Blazefield Travel in April 2001. Two months later its Portuguese operation was sold to ScottURB. Then, during the following year, it sold its SunBus school bus operations in Queensland, Australia, and exited the country, while in December 2002 it disposed of some of its Coach USA services in north-east America to Peter Pan Bus Lines. Back in the UK, at the end of July and in early August Stagecoach was heavily involved in the provision of transport for the Commonwealth

Games in Manchester and added appropriate branding to the buses employed on special services to the stadium. Meanwhile, further buses to be acquired from Hong Kong Citybus in 2002 were tri-axle Leyland Olympians, which were placed in service with Stagecoach Manchester in its low-cost Magic Bus unit.

Continuing its overseas contraction, in June 2003 Stagecoach sold its Hong Kong Citybus operations to Chow Tai Fook Enterprises, the holding company of New World First Bus, as well as its Coach USA network of services in south-east America. Back at home, on 4 August it introduced its new megabus.com brand with a service from London to Oxford. megabus offered a new, low-cost form of express coach travel on which fares began at £1 plus a 50p booking fee (all tickets having to be purchased online) and steadily increased as seats filled up. Following its launch, in September megabus services began north of the border on services between Edinburgh and Perth and Glasgow and Dundee, and following their success other services were added across the UK. Initially the vehicles used by megabus were elderly double-deckers – mainly ex-Stagecoach Kenya Bus tri-axle Leyland Olympians, which were fitted with coach seats and painted in a dark blue livery, although some two-axle Olympians were added at a later date.

Steadily starting to embark on the acquisition trail again, in July 2004 Stagecoach purchased the Glasgow to Edinburgh express M8 Motorvator service from Lanarkshire-based Longs Coaches and continued to use the Motorvator branding and red and cream livery until 13 September 2005, when Stagecoach entered into a joint agreement with Scottish Citylink. Later, in September 2004, Stagecoach purchased the remainder of Phil Anslow Travel, adding a further six minibuses and fifteen coaches to its Red & White subsidiary. Meanwhile, Stagecoach had begun to add route branding to some of its buses, although this was applied to the existing corporate livery and less flamboyantly than the schemes adopted by some other operators.

In comparison with the previous few years, 2005 proved to be a very busy one, starting on 31 March with the purchase of Dukinfield-based Dennis's Coaches, who operated two local bus services between Ashton-under-Lyne and Manchester in competition with Stagecoach-owned GM Buses South, to whose fleet several of its buses were added. Then, on 12 July, Stagecoach gained its first major foothold in Merseyside when it purchased Glenvale Transport Limited (GTL) after failing to purchase the Gillmoss depot and its operations from Arriva in 2000. Inheriting 180 buses, a large number of which were former London Leyland Titans and MCW Metrobuses, Stagecoach quickly began to replace these with new buses, with the last Titans being withdrawn in February 2006. As mentioned earlier, on 13 September 2005 Stagecoach entered into a joint venture with ComfortDelGro-owned Scottish Citylink, in which it took a 35 per cent stake, thus ending the long-running competition between the two companies. To this end, Stagecoach repainted a number of its coaches into Citylink livery, together with its branding. Later in the year, on 21 November, Stagecoach sold all its New Zealand operations to Infratil, who rebranded them NZ Bus, and thus completed its exit from the southern hemisphere. Back in the UK, however, expansion was achieved again on 14 December when Stagecoach purchased the Yorkshire Traction Group, whose operations were based in South Yorkshire, Lincolnshire and eastern Scotland.

These comprised Yorkshire Traction, Barnsley & District, Lincolnshire Road Car and Strathtay Scottish, bringing Stagecoach into new areas of England and further strengthening its position in eastern Scotland.

Soon after 2006 began, Stagecoach Red & White further reduced competition in the Welsh eastern valleys when it purchased Crosskeys-based Glyn Williams Travel and moved its acquired vehicles into its own Crosskeys depot. More surprisingly, however, in August it sold its East London and Selkent operations and buses to Australian Macquarie Bank. This took Stagecoach out of the capital after twelve years of providing TfL contracted services on both sides of the Thames. Meanwhile, across the Atlantic Stagecoach Coach USA introduced megabus.com on a network of services based on Chicago, thus giving American travellers the opportunity of low-cost coach travel. After gaining a substantial number of county council tenders back home, Stagecoach Devon expanded its local fleet and opened new depots at Barnstaple, Bude and Torrington to cater for its new services.

The year 2007 got underway with Stagecoach's purchase, in February, of the Stratford Blue operations and depot of Purfleet-based Ensignbus to give it some local bus services and open-top sightseeing tours, which Ensign had itself gained from Guide Friday in May 2002. In the summer, Stagecoach strengthened its position in South West England when it acquired the sixty-bus, Wellington-based Cooks Coaches, who operated a number of tendered services in its home town, Honiton, Chard and Exeter. Then, it turned its attention to railed transport when, on 7 July, it gained a ten-year contract to operate Transport for Greater Manchester's Metrolink tramway services. Later in the year, on 11 November, it was both winner and loser when it lost its Virgin CrossCountry railway franchise (in which it held a 49 per cent stake) to Arriva Trains, but it gained a new rail franchise – East Midland Trains – which had been created from Midland Mainline and the Midlands section of the Central Trains franchise. Meanwhile, after causing the demise of municipally owned Darlington Transport in November 1994, due to a decline in passenger numbers Stagecoach withdrew from the town on 26 August when it sold its operations, depot and twenty-eight Dennis Darts to Arriva North East. Then, in November, Stagecoach added Stagecoach Gold to its portfolio, this being designed to attract more middle-class passengers to use the bus rather than their cars. The buses employed were fitted with free Wi-Fi and leather seats, and were painted in a gold livery, with the first being operated in Perth and Warwick before being rolled out in several other parts of the UK.

Moving forward in time, 2008 proved to be a very busy year for Stagecoach, starting on 27 January when it purchased the bus operations (and thirty-eight buses) of Manchester independent A. Mayne & Son to further reduce competition on the Ashton corridor, although Mayne's retained its coaching activities, with these not being included in the deal. Following this, on 31 March, Stagecoach acquired Cambridgeshire-based Cavalier Contracts, who also operated as Huntingdon & District, thus returning the Scottish group to a town in which it had a depot until its forced sale, together with Milton Keynes Citybus, by the Office of Fair Trading in 1997. This gave Stagecoach access to the proposed Cambridgeshire Guided Busway, which, following numerous delays, did not open until 7 August 2011. On 28 March Stagecoach Fife purchased

Rennies of Dunfermline and its sixty-vehicle fleet, of which eighteen were double-deck buses used on contract duties. Unusually, Stagecoach retained Rennies as a separate company with its own livery, which is still being maintained in 2018. Due to being out on a limb from its main area of operation, in May Stagecoach subsidiary Yorkshire Traction sold its Huddersfield depot and resident vehicles to Centrebus Holdings Ltd – a company formed by Centrebus and Arriva. Also, on the 16th of that same month, Stagecoach Highland purchased Rapson's Highland Country Buses and Orkney Coaches Ltd, together with around 200 buses and coaches, to further consolidate its position in the north of Scotland and give it services on Orkney. Then, on 10 August, Stagecoach eliminated more of its competition along Wilmslow Road, Manchester, when it purchased the commercial bus operations of Bullocks of Cheadle, who retained its coaching activities, its school bus contracts and the 147 service from Manchester Piccadilly to the city's hospitals along Oxford Road. Later that month, on the 29th, Stagecoach introduced a trial ferry service in Devon from Torquay to Brixham using a 138-seat catamaran, although this did not prove as successful as had been hoped and ceased operation on 27 September. Then, shortly before the year closed, Stagecoach acquired municipally owned Eastbourne Buses Ltd together with its forty-nine buses, and took control on 18 December. In the meantime, on 22 June, Stagecoach USA withdrew from Los Angeles and California and instead gave greater concentration to its operations in America's north-east.

After another busy year, 2009 started with a bang when, in January, Stagecoach further consolidated its position in Eastbourne with its purchase of local independent Cavendish Motor Services, a sister company of Renown Coaches of Bexhill. Three months later, Cavendish's services were merged with those acquired with Eastbourne Buses. Of greater importance was Stagecoach's acquisition on 23 January of former municipal Preston Bus from its management owners. However, after this takeover was referred to the Competition Commission, Stagecoach was instructed to operate Preston Bus at arm's length from the main Stagecoach business and restore its livery and logo to its buses before ultimately being instructed in November 2009 to sell the company, which it did on 19 January 2011 when it disposed of it to Rotala plc. Following its success with its low-cost megabusplus.com operations, on 30 March Stagecoach launched megabusplus on some of its services from East Lancashire and Yorkshire to London. These used coaches to travel to East Midlands Parkway railway station, where passengers were then transferred onto East Midland Trains for the remainder of their journey to London St Pancras. Following its growing success in the USA towards the end of the year, Stagecoach Canada introduced megabus.com to its long-distance service network with a mixture of single- and double-deck coaches.

On the first day of 2010, Stagecoach Red & White further strengthened its position in south-east Wales when it purchased Pontllanfraith-based, municipally owned Islwyn Borough Transport and its thirty-three buses. Then on 10 October, to great surprise, Stagecoach repurchased its former East London and Selkent companies from Macquarie Bank to give it a major presence in the English capital once again.

The year 2011 proved to be another one of consolidation, with Stagecoach selling its franchise to operate Manchester's Metrolink tramway to RATP in August. As one door closed, another opened, however, and in October Stagecoach began a megabus.com overnight sleeper service from London to Glasgow using two of its bendicoaches, which were fitted with bunks. As on other megabus.com services, the fare started at £1 plus a 50p booking fee, rising to £40 for the last few places. Then, just before the year ended, Stagecoach South bought the twenty-two-bus Countrywide Travel, who traded as Fleet Buzz. They initially maintained it as a separate business, retaining its yellow livery.

While 2012 was another comparatively quiet year in Stagecoach terms, the group was heavily involved in the provision of transport for the Olympic Games in London at the end of July and early August. As contracted providers of transport for the athletes and members of the media, Stagecoach brought in a large number of buses and coaches – and employees – from its various subsidiaries across the UK, and as a condition of its contract, all fleet and manufacturer's identities had to be removed from the vehicles used, although several were seen to escape from this edict. Despite this being a major exercise, Stagecoach undertook its duties admirably in every respect and could be justifiably proud of itself. Meanwhile, earlier in the year, on 16 April, Stagecoach launched some megabus.com services from the UK to mainland Europe, running from Birmingham to Paris and Brussels, and started a service from Paris to Brussels and Amsterdam, all using the ferry from Dover or Ramsgate. Then, on 2 December, Stagecoach surprisingly purchased First Manchester's Wigan depot, its operations and 120 buses, of which twenty were owned by Transport for Greater Manchester.

Continuing on the acquisition trail, on 13 January 2013 Stagecoach purchased First Group's Chester operations, and depots in the city and at Rock Ferry, together with 110 buses, as well as its school bus operation and small depot at Wrexham. This took Stagecoach onto the Wirral peninsula for the first time and gave it a strong foothold in Cheshire. Following this, Stagecoach further strengthened its position in Greater Manchester when, on 3 March, it purchased Middleton-based independent operator Bluebird, together with its depot and modern fleet of forty buses. Then, four months later, Stagecoach introduced a new megabus Gold overnight sleeper service from London to Edinburgh and Aberdeen, for which a fleet of new, luxurious tri-axle Van Hool double-deck coaches were bought. Later in the year, on 21 October, megabus.com began a new service from London to Cologne, taking it into Germany for the first time, and also launched a new service from the UK to Antwerp and Rotterdam. In connection with these, Stagecoach purchased ten left-hand drive Van Hool coaches to complement its existing UK megabus fleet. Finally, on 17 December, Stagecoach acquired the operations and seventy-four-bus fleet of King's Lynn-based independent Norfolk Green, surprisingly retaining its livery and identity for over twelve months.

During the following year, on 26 April 2014, Stagecoach continued its elimination of competition in Greater Manchester when it purchased the operations and forty-one-bus fleet of Middleton-based independent JPT Bus Company, moving it into its nearby former Bluebird depot. Then megabus was in the news again when it began a service from London to Paris and Barcelona, taking it into Spain for the first time, as well as launching a service within Germany from Cologne to Munich.

Moving into 2015, the first event of note was Stagecoach winning the railway franchise for the East Coast Main Line in partnership with Virgin, who held a

10 per cent stake, with Stagecoach having the remaining 90 per cent. Stagecoach took over the electrified operation (from state-owned Directly Operated Railways, who had taken it over from National Express in November 2009) under the title Virgin Trains East Coast on 1 March. Following this, on 24 June, megabus Europe spread its wings in Italy, where it obtained a depot at Bergamo. From here it launched five internal services that spread between Venice and Rome. Later, on 8 July, a service from London to Milan was started, thus connecting the UK to Italy for the first time. Then, back in the UK, on 6 September Stagecoach purchased First Devon and Cornwall's operations and depot at Plymouth, as well as its outstations at Dartmouth and Tavistock, further strengthening its position in South West England.

On 1 July 2016, Stagecoach somewhat surprisingly sold its megabus operations on mainland Europe, as well as its services linking London with Europe, to its German competitor, Flixbus. Stagecoach continued as a contractor, however, so initially no route changes were made, although this ultimately altered with megabus ceasing its mainland Europe activities and returning its left-hand drive coaches to the UK, where they were placed in storage.

Although megabus.com continued to expand in the UK during 2017 with the introduction of new services, its megabus Gold sleeper operation had sadly not proved to be viable, and as a result was discontinued in May. However, on the first day of the same month, it entered into a partnership with South Gloucestershire Bus & Coach Co. to allow its services – Barnstaple to Nottingham; Barnstaple to London via Bristol and Heathrow Airport; Cardiff to Heathrow and Gatwick airports; and Gloucester to London – to be operated under the megabus.com banner using twenty-six coaches, some of which had been transferred from megabus's left-hand drive reserve fleet. Later in the year, on 29 September, megabus entered into a similar partnership with Aberystwyth-based Mid Wales Travel for the latter to operate the Friday, Saturday and Sunday M39 service from Aberystwyth to London via Cardiff service with its own coach, which would carry megabus branding. Meanwhile, Stagecoach had lost its franchise to operate South West Trains when this passed, on 20 August, to South Western Railway – a joint venture between First Group and MTR Europe.

After viewing London's ever-expanding sightseeing tours market, on 23 April 2018 Stagecoach launched a low-price operation under the megasightseeing.com banner, with fares starting at £1 plus a 50p booking fee. With non-stop, two-hour tours departing every hour from three different locations across London, these are maintained with megabus blue-liveried, ex-Stagecoach London, Dennis Tridents, which have been converted to full or part open-top configuration. Then, two months later, as a result of overbidding for the East Coast Main Line railway operation (which was maintained under the Virgin Trains East Coast banner), Stagecoach sadly ceased its operation on 23 June 2018 and handed it back to the Department for Transport, who continued it under the LNER name. Finally, on 25 October 2018, Stagecoach commenced operation of the UK's first Tram Trains, this being a two-year trial using the Sheffield Supertram track from Sheffield to Meadowhall, at which point the dual-voltage trams continue along the national rail network lines to Rotherham.

As can be seen from the above, despite disposing of all its overseas operations, except those in North America and Canada where it operates 2,400 coaches, Stagecoach has continued to grow in the UK throughout the twenty-first century, now employing around 8,500 buses and coaches. Undoubtedly Stagecoach will continue to expand whenever, and wherever, opportunities arise, and will also continue in its bid to further minimise the impact of its operations on the environment with an increase in alternatively powered buses such as hybrid, gas, hydrogen and electric.

Without the help of others for allowing me to use their excellent photographs, there would have been numerous gaps in the pictorial content of this book, and thus I offer my most sincere thanks to all those who have assisted. The photographs that are uncredited are from my own camera, while those whose identity is unfortunately unknown to me are shown as author's collection. To the latter I apologise profusely and hope that they will forgive me for using their work, but will nevertheless enjoy seeing it in print, as without these the pictorial history would have been incomplete. Their contribution is thus greatly appreciated.

Seen lined up in the yard of Stagecoach Midland Red's Leamington Spa depot on 14 September 2000 are five ECW-bodied Leyland Olympians cascaded from Stagecoach Selkent, a Northern Counties-bodied Volvo Olympian that also began life with Selkent, and a Dodge G13 driver trainer.

Heading through Blackheath on its way to Lewisham on 4 June 2000 is Stagecoach Selkent Plaxton-bodied Mercedes-Benz O814D MB18 (R518 YWC).

Seen wearing East London Coaches fleet names is Plaxton Paramount 3500-bodied Volvo B10M VP1 (WLT 890), which carried a former Stagecoach Routemaster registration number.

Heading a line of Alexander-bodied Dennis Dominators is Allison of Dunfermline's MWB 855W, which still wears the livery of its former owner, Sheffield Mainline. (Author's collection)

New to Northern Scottish, Alexander-bodied Leyland Tiger D744 BRS is seen here in Stagecoach's JW Coaches fleet. (Author's collection)

New to Alexander Fife, Duple-bodied Leyland PSU3E/4R GSG 127T is seen here at Heysham Travel's depot together with the company's ex-Merseybus Alexander-bodied Leyland AN68C/1R 1886 (XEM 886W) – both of which passed to Stagecoach Lancaster with the Heysham Travel business.

Seen in Newport bus station is Phil Anslow's UVG-bodied Iveco 59.12 P974 UKG. (D. P. B. Davies)

Seen in Stockport on 22 May 2000 while operating both versions of route 192 are Stagecoach Manchester Magic Bus-liveried Northern Counties-bodied Leyland Olympian 3087 (B87 SJA), which began life with Greater Manchester PTE, and corporate-liveried Alexander-bodied Dennis Trident 619 (V619 DJA).

Parked outside Stagecoach Cumberland's Barrow depot is a line of Alexander-bodied Leyland Olympians headed by 14246 (F806 FAO), behind which is an example repainted into the new corporate livery.

Illustrating Stagecoach's old and new liveries are Alexander-bodied MAN 18.220s 22233 (X233 BNE) and 22132 (S132 TRJ), both seen in service with Stagecoach Manchester in their home city on 2 August 2002.

Stagecoach in the Twenty-First Century 15

New to Thames Transit but seen here in Canterbury after being cascaded to Stagecoach East Kent is Alexander-bodied Volvo Olympian 16503 (R503 UWL).

Seen outside Stagecoach Cumberland's Barrow depot with several of its sisters is Alexander (Belfast)-bodied Mercedes-Benz 709D 40646 (N646 VSS), which started life with Stagecoach Manchester.

With 'Air Conditioned Quality' lettering at each side of its destination screen, Stagecoach Coastline Plaxton-bodied Dennis Dart 435 (405 DCD), seen here in Portsmouth, was originally operated by Stagecoach Hong Kong Citybus. (F. W. York)

Collecting its passengers in Colne bus station on 18 April 2001 while wearing Stagecoach's old corporate livery and Burnley & Pendle's fleet names is Plaxton-bodied Dennis Javelin 949 (M949 JBO), which had started life seven years earlier with Red & White.

Stagecoach in the Twenty-First Century

New to Greater Manchester PTE, Stagecoach Burnley & Pendle MCW Metrobus 1225 (SND 120X) starts loading in Burnley bus station on 18 April 2001 while operating the local service to Stoops Estate.

Seen at East Didsbury on 15 May 2002 when only a few days old is Stagecoach Manchester Alexander-bodied Dennis Trident 1627 (MK02 EGV), which has been painted into a special livery to commemorate Queen Elizabeth II's Golden Jubilee. Standing behind it is another of the company's Dennis Tridents, this time wearing the old corporate livery.

Awaiting passengers attending the Commonwealth Games on 2 August 2002, Stagecoach Manchester Alexander-bodied Dennis Trident 1619 (MX02 EFY) has additional route information on its destination screen and lower side panels.

Resting at Stagecoach's Blochairn depot, Glasgow on 12 October 2003 are megabus-liveried Alexander-bodied Leyland Olympian 14237 (G337 KKW) which was new to Stagecoach East Midland and Alexander-bodied tri-axle Leyland Olympians 14239/40 (WLT 727/794), which began life with Stagecoach Cumberland, registered F201/2FHH. As can be seen, 14239/40 carry Glasgow – Edinburgh lettering on their lower side panels.

Approaching Manchester Piccadilly bus station on 19 November 2004 is Stagecoach Manchester Magic Bus-liveried Alexander-bodied tri-axle Leyland Olympian 13503 (C42 HNF), which had been imported from Kowloon Motor Bus, Hong, Kong in whose fleet it was registered DH 9398.

Seen at Aviemore depot wearing a dedicated livery for the Cairngorms National Park shuttle is Stagecoach Highlands Alexander PS-bodied Volvo Blom 20570 (M470 ASW). (Richard Walter)

About to leave Buchanan bus station, Glasgow, on its journey to Edinburgh, is Stagecoach Plaxton-bodied Volvo B10M M161 CDD, which was new to Stagecoach South. It is seen here wearing Motorvator livery with its Stagecoach identity above its front wheel arch, and megabus.com lettering above its door.

Collecting its Ashton-under-Lyne-bound passengers in Piccadilly, Manchester, in 2002 is Dukinfield-based independent Dennis's East Lancs-bodied Dennis Trident X792 JHG.

Stagecoach Manchester East Lancs-bodied Dennis Trident 17649 (X792 JHG) was inherited with the Dennis's of Dukinfield business in March 2005. (M. H. A. Flynn)

Heading through Liverpool city centre are GTL Leyland Titan 2374 (KYV 374X) and MCW Metrobus 522 (GYE 522W), both of which started life with London Buses.

Still retaining the livery of CMT Buses after that company had been purchased by GTL, Alexander-bodied Volvo B10B 2073 (M392 VXW), which was new to Harrogate & District, is seen here heading through Liverpool city centre.

Resting in the yard of Stagecoach Western Buses' Kilmarnock depot is former London Leyland Titan 10473 (KYV 473X), painted in dedicated yellow School Bus livery. (Michael Young)

Still sporting Barnsley & District fleet names, Stagecoach Yorkshire Alexander-bodied Volvo B6 L651 OWY, seen here in Barnsley in February 2006, was new to Harrogate & District. (B. Newsome)

Still in the livery of their former owner, Yorkshire Traction, but sporting Stagecoach Yorkshire fleet names, are Northern Counties-bodied Volvo Olympian 16874 (P915 RYO), which began life with London General, and Wright-bodied Scania K93CRB 28756 (K276 EWA). The pair are seen here in the yard of their owner's Huddersfield depot in May 2006.

Leaving Huddersfield bus station in June 2006 on the X62 service to Leeds is Stagecoach Yorkshire Northern Counties-bodied Dennis Dart 32928 (N432 CHL), which was acquired with the business of Yorkshire Traction.

Seen in Grimsby is Road Car Alexander-bodied Leyland Olympian 653 (L603 NOS), which had been acquired by the Yorkshire Traction group with the Sheffield Omnibus business.

Pictured at Skegness after being converted to open-top configuration is Road Car MCW Metrobus 741 (WOI 3001), which began life with West Midlands PTE registered POG 571Y. (B. Newsome)

Resting between duties in Dundee in February 2006 is Stagecoach-owned Strathtay's East Lancs-bodied Dennis Dart SPD 314 (V314 DSL). (B. Newsome)

Fresh from the paint shop on 14 January 2006 after receiving corporate Stagecoach livery, but sporting Strathtay fleet names, is East Lancs-bodied Volvo Olympian 956 (R596 TSL). (Michael Young)

Seen in Newport bus station is Crosskeys-based Glyn Williams' UVG-bodied Dennis Dart SLF R424 AOR, which, together with the Williams business, passed to Stagecoach Red & White, by whom it was given fleet number 33278.

Displaying its owner's new-style fleet name is traditional-liveried Stagecoach East London AEC Routemaster RML886 (TAS 418), which was originally registered WLT 886.

Sporting a gold Stagecoach East London fleet name and cream window surrounds, former Green Line AEC Routemaster RMC1485 (485 CLT) is seen on Oxford Street, London, on 18 May 2003 while heading to Blackwall station.

Negotiating traffic on London's Oxford Street on 10 March 2005 is Stagecoach East London Mercedes-Benz 530G bendibus 23059 (LX04 LBP).

Standing at London City Airport on 5 June 2000 are Stagecoach East London Alexander-bodied Dennis Dart SLFs SLD33 (R933 FOO) and LCY6 (P806 NJN), both of which wear dedicated liveries for the two shuttle bus services to the terminal.

Circumnavigating Parliament Square on its way to Trafalgar Square on 17 May 2003, Stagecoach Selkent Alexander-bodied Dennis Trident 17274 (X274 NNO) shows off its owner's then London livery with blue skirt and blue and orange swoops.

Stagecoach Yorkshire Alexander-bodied tri-axle Leyland Olympian 13601 (BIW4977), seen here in Barnsley on 24 December 2008, had previously been part of the megabus fleet but had begun life with Hong Kong Citybus, registered as ER 9371. (M. Quiney)

Repainted in corporate livery, Stagecoach Yorkshire East Lancs-bodied DAF SB220 26115 (X215 HHE), seen leaving Huddersfield bus station, was one of the buses inherited with the Yorkshire Traction business.

Making its way along Park Lane, London, on 10 March 2005 is Stagecoach Thames Transit's Oxford Tube-liveried Neoplan Skyliner 50102 (KP04 GJF).

Typifying Stagecoach's large fleet of Alexander-bodied Dennis Tridents is Stagecoach Swindon's 18448 (VU06 JDZ) seen here in its home town on 18 September 2013. (T. S. Blackman)

Stagecoach in the Twenty-First Century 31

New to London Buses in February 1993, but seen here with Stagecoach Cheltenham District, is Wright Handybus-bodied Dennis Dart 32234 (NDZ 3134). (B. Newsome)

Seen at its launch in Chicago is Stagecoach megabus.com USA's as yet unregistered Van Hool Astromega DD562. (Stagecoach)

Seen leaving Buchanan bus station, Glasgow, is Stagecoach West Scotland Jonckheere-bodied Volvo B10MA bendibus 51094 (T642 KCS).

With route branding on its cove panels and across its windows is Stagecoach Cheltenham District Optare Solo 47557 (VX57 NZZ). (Gawan Wood)

Stagecoach in the Twenty-First Century

Posed for a publicity photograph, and displaying fictitious registration plate B10 PSV, Stagecoach West Scotland bio-fuelled Alexander-bodied MAN 18.220 22601 (V601 GCS) was given a corporate-style environmentally friendly livery. (Stagecoach)

Repainted into the old Western SMT coach livery, Stagecoach West Scotland Plaxton-bodied Volvo B10M 52359 (P159 ASA) is seen here at Kilmarnock depot on 7 May 2007. (Michael Young)

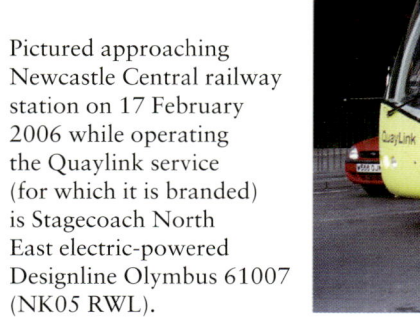

Pictured approaching Newcastle Central railway station on 17 February 2006 while operating the Quaylink service (for which it is branded) is Stagecoach North East electric-powered Designline Olympus 61007 (NK05 RWL).

Seen when comparatively new in 2004 is Stagecoach United Counties East Lancs-bodied Scania N94UD 15401 (KX04 RCV), which has been painted in Corby Star livery. (Author's collection)

Stagecoach United Counties used the names of satellites for many of its services in and around Bedford. Here, Northern Counties-bodied Volvo Olympian 16674 (L674 HNV) is seen branded for the Pluto service from Bedford to Northampton. (R. G. Pope)

Stagecoach in the Twenty-First Century 35

Several of Hampshire's rural bus services have been operated under the Cango banner since 2003. Suitably branded Stagecoach South Optare Solo 47419 (YJ05 XMS), which began life with Wilts & Dorset, is seen here operating the 22 service to Burghclere. (T. S. Blackman)

Displaying a Stagecoach Sheffield fleet name, Stagecoach Yorkshire Alexander-bodied MAN 18.220 22432 (YN07 KRE), seen here on 23 May 2007 when only a month old, is adorned with branding for the frequent 88 service, which runs across Sheffield through the city centre.

Wearing West Yorkshire PTE 'My Bus' branding and Yorkshire Traction fleet names, Stagecoach Yorkshire BMC 1100FE yellow school bus 29704 (YN05 WEA) stands in the yard of its owner's since-closed Shafton depot on 9 May 2007.

A member of South West Trains' railway replacement fleet, Stagecoach South Alexander-bodied tri-axle Leyland Olympian 13620 (H723 KDY) had been acquired from Stagecoach's Hong Kong Citybus, in whose fleet it was registered ER 6587. (F. W. York)

Stagecoach in the Twenty-First Century 37

Seen in Canterbury bus station on 2 July 2012 while wearing a branded livery for the service to the University of Kent is Stagecoach East Kent Alexander-bodied Dennis Trident 18529 (GX06 DYT). (M. H. A. Flynn)

New to London Buses, Northern Counties-bodied Leyland Olympian 14925 (E925 KYR), with a Stagecoach in Hull fleet name, is seen here operating a local service in its home city on 14 November 2005.

With a fixed destination display for Hull's 703 Park & Ride service, Stagecoach Hull Alexander-bodied Mercedes-Benz 0814D 42358 (S358 KEF), which began life with Cleveland Transit, rests at Hedon, Hull, on 14 November 2005.

New to Cleveland Transit, Stagecoach in Sunderland's immaculately presented Leyland Lynx 2 29629 (K629 YVN) makes its way through its home city on 30 May 2007.

Painted in Blue Solos livery for operation on Bedfordshire County Council funded services, Stagecoach United Counties Optare Solo 47440 (YJ56 AOP) is seen here en route to Goldington on route 4. (R. G. Pope)

Wearing Taunton Flyer-branded livery, Stagecoach South West Optare Solo 47590 (YJ55 BHN) was one of the buses taken over with the Cooks of Wellington business. (T. W. W. Knowles)

Heading along Mosley Street, Manchester, is Metrolink AlsaldoBreda T-68 2-module articulated tram No. 1002, which was new in 1992.

Seen here at Matlock, East Midlands Trains' two-car diesel Super Sprinter No. 156414 was built by Metro-Cammell, and dates from 1987. (M. H. A. Flynn)

Stagecoach in the Twenty-First Century

Travelling down Tubwell Row, Darlington on 30 May 2007, Stagecoach Darlington Alexander-bodied Dennis Dart 32637 (P637 PGP), which began life in London with Selkent, overtakes Arriva Optare MetroRider P616 FHN, which was new to United. Three months later, 32637 would pass to Arriva Durham County along with Stagecoach's Darlington operations.

Repainted into Cheltenham District livery in 2009 to commemorate the company's 80th anniversary, Stagecoach Cheltenham District Plaxton-bodied Dennis Dart 33506 (X509 ADF) is seen here in its home surroundings. (Gawan Wood)

Standing side by side in Bicester on 28 September 2013 are Stagecoach Oxford coach-seated Alexander Dennis-bodied Scania N230UDs 15758/60 (OU61 AVN/AVP), both wearing Stagecoach Gold livery. (T. S. Blackman)

Seen in Piccadilly, Manchester, with 'Easy Access Bus' lettering on its lower side panels, is independent Mayne's East Lancs-bodied Dennis Trident 25 (V125 DJA). (B. Newsome)

Stagecoach in the Twenty-First Century

Still wearing the livery of its previous owner, Manchester independent Mayne, but now with Stagecoach fleet names, Northern Counties-bodied Scania N113DRB 15382 (G115 SBA) prepares to leave Piccadilly bus station, Manchester, on the 42 service to East Didsbury on 11 September 2008. (M. H. A. Flynn)

Two of Stagecoach Manchester's East Lancs-bodied Scania N113DRBs, 15382 (M210NDB) and 15381 (L114 DNA), acquired with the Mayne business, show off their new owner's corporate livery in September 2008. It is interesting to see that the destination blind on 15381 reads 'Clayton Mayne Garage'. (K. S. E. Till)

Resting in Huntingdon bus station is Cavalier Alexander-bodied Leyland Olympian 4222 (A978 OST), which started life in Scotland with Highland Omnibuses. (B. Newsome)

Devoid of fleet names, but retaining Huntingdon & District livery, is Cavalier Contracts' much-travelled ECW-bodied Leyland Olympian B264 LPH, which was new to London Country and later operated with Keighley & District.

Seen at Showbus in September 2012 wearing Cambridgeshire Guided Busway-branded livery are Stagecoach in the Fens Wright-bodied Volvo B7RLE 21233 (AE12 CJU) and Alexander Dennis-bodied Scania N230UD 15814 (AE12 CKK). (T. S. Blackman)

Stagecoach Rennies 29861 (BU06 NZU) was an Autosan Eagle purchased new when the Dunfermline-based company was still independent. (Richard Walter)

Collecting a large number of passengers in Piccadilly, Manchester, on 29 July 2008 is Stagecoach Manchester's Magic Bus-liveried Alexander-bodied Volvo B10M 20935 (R935 XVM). (M. H. A. Flynn)

New to Ulsterbus, Plaxton-bodied Volvo B10M DAZ 1571 was later purchased by Scottish independent Rapsons, in whose livery, with Orkney fleet name, it is seen here at Aviemore on 26 June 2009. This was after it had passed to Stagecoach, whose identity and fleet number, 52201, are seen on its front panel. (Murdoch Currie)

Passing Christie Hospital, Manchester, shortly before being acquired by Stagecoach, is Cheadle independent Bullock's East Lancs-bodied Scania N113DRB W675 PTD. (M. H. A. Flynn)

Passing through Stockport bus station in February 2009 after being repainted into corporate Stagecoach Manchester livery is former Bullock of Cheadle's East Lance-bodied Scania N113DRB 18283 (W673 PTD). (M. H. A. Flynn)

Stagecoach Manchester's former Bullock of Cheadle East Lance-bodied Dennis Trident 18293 (X939 NBU) is seen here after being repainted into Magic Bus livery. (M. H. A. Flynn)

Eastbourne Buses Northern Counties-bodied DAF SB220 126 (P906 PWW) started life with Speedlink Services. (Showbus)

Seen while operating a town service in Eastbourne for Cavendish Motor Services is sister company Renown Travel's Plaxton-bodied Dennis Dart 67 (M97 WBW), which began life with Thames Transit. (T. S. Blackman)

Leaving Preston bus station on 26 January 2009, and displaying Preston Bus and Stagecoach fleet names, is East Lancs Esteem-bodied Scania K230UB 202 (PRN 909), which started life registered as PL06 RYP.

Acquired by Preston Bus from Lothian Buses, Alexander-bodied Leyland Olympian 132 (E332 MSG) is seen here in Preston bus station on 26 January 2009 wearing Stagecoach fleet names three days after the former municipal operator was taken over.

Seen in Montreal, Canada, with a Stagecoach fleet name on its front upper deck side panel, open-top AEC Routemaster 709 had been acquired from Stagecoach East London in March 2005, in whose fleet it was numbered RML2709 and registered SMK 709F. (Author's collection)

Displaying 'A Stagecoach Group Company' title above its front wheel arch, Coach Canada Provost H3-45 83809 is seen here awaiting its passengers in Toronto. (Author's collection)

Stagecoach in the Twenty-First Century

51

With a Stagecoach banner across its door ready for the December 2009 launch of Chesterfield's new Castleline services, for which it is branded, is Stagecoach East Midland Alexander Dennis-bodied MAN 18.240 22645 (YN58 CEV). (Stagecoach)

Seen in Canterbury bus station on 22 August 2012, adorned with branding for the Breeze service to Broadstairs, is Stagecoach East Kent Alexander Dennis-bodied Scania N230UD 15491 (GN09 BBO). (M. H. A. Flynn)

Seen displaying a route map and Lakes Rider branding on its side panels on 20 August 2008 is Stagecoach North West open-top Leyland Titan 10281 (GYE 281W), which had migrated north from Stagecoach East London to A1 Service, Ardrossan, in January 1995, before being transferred to Cumbria in September 2000. (M. H. A. Flynn)

Painted in Traws Cambria dedicated livery and seen heading here to Brecon is Stagecoach Red & White Optare Tempo 25101 (YJ55 YFY). (Richard Walter)

Awaiting its passengers at Bicester on 28 September 2013 is Stagecoach United Counties Plaxton-bodied Volvo B9R 53611 (KX58 NCD), which wears branding for the half-hourly X5 service from Oxford to Cambridge. (T. S. Blackman)

Adorned with an overall advert, except for its front panels, is Stagecoach Devon Reeve Burgess-bodied Mercedes-Benz 709D 425 (F743FDV), which was new to Devon General. It is seen here in Exeter in 2000 standing alongside former Stagecoach London Leyland Titan 953 (NUW 644Y). (T. W. W. Knowles)

Wearing an all-over Hovertravel promotional livery, Stagecoach South Alexander-bodied Dennis Dart 33156 (LK55 KZZ), seen here at the Hard Interchange, Portsmouth, began life with Classic Coaches at Annfield Plain. (F. W. York)

On loan to Stagecoach Grimsby-Cleethorpes during its shortage of buses, Stagecoach East London Northern Counties-bodied Volvo Olympian VN174 (R174HHK) is seen here on service in Grimsby on 24 October 2002.

Having just left Buchanan bus station, Glasgow, at the start of its journey to St Andrews on 24 April 2009, Stagecoach Fife Plaxton-bodied Volvo B7R 53283 (SP07 HHL) carries Express City Connect branding on its side panels. (Murdoch Currie)

Heading though the Bradford suburb of Odsal on 9 September 2009 on the megabusplus.com MP1 service is Stagecoach East Midlands Plaxton-bodied Volvo B10M 52310 (N619 USS), which had begun life in Scotland with Stagecoach Bluebird.

Seen in Caerphilly is Islwyn Borough Transport Optare Solo 11 (YJ58 BZX). (Author's collection)

With a hybrid logo on its lower side panels, Stagecoach East London Alexander Dennis E40H 12149 (LX61 DCU) is pictured here on TfL route 15 on 25 November 2012. (T. S. Blackman)

Seen in its home town, branded for the Popin 6 service on 18 September 2013, is Stagecoach Swindon & District Alexander Dennis Enviro200 36126 (VX10 COA). (T. S. Blackman)

Painted in Stagecoach's corporate-style hybrid livery, and carrying Electric Hybrid lettering on its upper deck side panels, is Stagecoach Manchester Alexander-bodied Dennis Trident 12045 (MX60 BVM), seen here en route to Stockport on 17 February 2011. (L. J. Long)

Converted to a sleeper coach, for which it carries lettering on its side panels, is Stagecoach megabus.com Jonckheere-bodied Volvo B10MA bendicoach 51097 (T97 JHN), which started life with Stagecoach Cleveland Transit. (Malcolm Crowe)

Still wearing Fleet Buzz livery, but displaying Stagecoach fleet number 25249, is Optare Versa MX09 AOK. (Author's collection)

Stagecoach in the Twenty-First Century

Seen in Waterloo Street, Glasgow, on 8 March 2012, Stagecoach West Scotland Plaxton-bodied tri-axle Volvo B13RT 54108 (SF61 EYP) collects its passengers on the X76 service to Kilmarnock and Irvine, for which it is branded. (Murdoch Currie)

Awaiting its departure from Shudehill Interchange, Manchester, on 20 October 2012 is Stagecoach Bluebird megabus.com-liveried Van Hool TDX27 50249 (SV62 BDX). It is heading to London on the Anglo-Scottish M11 service. (M. H. A. Flynn)

Proudly displaying 'Travel the Bluebird' lettering on its side panels, Stagecoach Bluebird Plaxton-bodied Volvo B7R 53266 (SV56 BVW) is seen here at Inverness Retail Park on 22 May 2012. (Murdoch Currie)

Pictured in High Street, Ayr, on 22 October 2012 when only a few days old, is Stagecoach West Scotland Alexander Dennis E20D 36745 (SF62CZL) wearing Asda Rider branding. (Murdoch Currie)

Stagecoach in the Twenty-First Century 61

A healthy load of passengers board Stagecoach North West's X2-branded Alexander Dennis-bodied Scania N230UD 15473 (PX09 AXC) in Liverpool on 3 March 2009. (L. J. Long)

Painted in a commemorative livery to celebrate the centenary of the erstwhile Aldershot & District is Stagecoach South Alexander Dennis-bodied MAN 14.240 39651 (GX08 HBN), seen here at Showbus in 2012. (T. S. Blackman)

Wearing biobus livery is Stagecoach West Scotland Alexander Dennis-bodied MAN 18.240 24187 (SF10 BYY) seen here leaving Kilmarnock bus station. (Murdoch Currie)

Stagecoach Hull Frequento-branded Transbus Trident 18030 (MX53 FLK), which was new to Stagecoach Manchester, is seen passing through Leeds on the X62 service, which uses the M62 motorway, on 17 March 2009.

With a promotional logo on its lower side panels and route branding above its side windows, Stagecoach North West Alexander Dennis Dart SLF 34709 (PX05 ENN) awaits time in English Street, Carlisle, on 2 June 2012. (Murdoch Currie)

Resting in Bridge Street, Wick, on 5 June 2012 is Stagecoach Highlands Van Hool-bodied Volvo B10M 52044 (200 UWX), which was new to Longs of Salsburgh, with whom it was registered M873 GYS. It later served with Rapsons, from whom Stagecoach acquired it. (Murdoch Currie)

Branded for the X99 service from Inverness to Scrabster, Stagecoach Highland Country Plaxton-bodied Volvo B9R 53624 (SV11 FFU) is seen here in Wick on 4 June 2012. (Murdoch Currie)

Immaculately presented in a past London Transport livery is Stagecoach Selkent Alexander Dennis E40D 10136 (LX12 DFN), which carries the name 'Selkent Ambassador' on its front upper deck side panel.

Painted in Stagecoach Gold livery, Stagecoach Fife hybrid Alexander Dennis E35H 29017 (SP12 DYT) stands at the Scone Park & Ride site on 24 August 2012. (Murdoch Currie)

Branded for the cross-Humber Fast Cat service from Scunthorpe to Hull, Stagecoach Lincolnshire Alexander Dennis-bodied MAN 18.240 22758 (FX09 DBV) is seen having just arrived at Scunthorpe bus station on 1 October 2014. (M. H. A. Flynn)

Seen at Scara Brae on 8 September 2012 while operating the Discover Orkney tour is Stagecoach Highlands open-top Northern Counties-bodied Volvo Olympian 16545 (P545 EFL) which began life with Cambus in closed top form. (John Sinclair)

Collecting passengers at Shude Hill Interchange, Manchester, while operating an Anglo-Scottish megabus service on 20 February 2013 is Stagecoach Glasgow Plaxton-bodied Volvo B11RT 54204 (SF62 CPU). (M. H. A. Flynn)

Branded for the X50 service, and with a red panel below its windscreen, Stagecoach Manchester Alexander Dennis Trident 19534 (MX09 KTV) is seen here in Manchester's Piccadilly bus station on 18 March 2013. (M. H. A. Flynn)

Stagecoach in the Twenty-First Century

MAN gas-propelled Caetano-bodied Ecocity A22 demonstrator WX61 FXO is seen here on 22 September 2011 while on loan to Stagecoach Merseyside. (L. J. Long)

Wearing an all-over livery to promote the service from Edinburgh city centre to the zoo is Stagecoach Neoplan Skyliner 50134 (511 OHU), which was new to Stagecoach Red & White for megabus.com duties as CN05 APX. It is seen here outside the zoo on 2 March 2012. (Murdoch Currie)

Branded for the 37 service, and seen in Stockton-on-Tees on 6 January 2013, is Stagecoach Transit Alexander-bodied MAN 18.240 24112 (NK09 FMD), which carries the name *Mr Snuggle Wuggle* above its front fleet name. (T. S. Blackman)

Seen in Inverness bus station on 24 March 2014 while painted in the old Northern Scottish livery is Stagecoach Bluebird Plaxton-bodied Volvo B7R 53334 (488 GWL), which was originally registered SV09 EFZ. (Murdoch Currie)

Stagecoach in the Twenty-First Century 69

Displaying 'Stagecoach celebrating the Queen's Jubilee' on its upper side panels is Stagecoach South Alexander-bodied Scania N230UD 15586 (GX59 JYT), pictured here on 16 September 2012. (T. S. Blackman)

Still displaying branding for Exeter's Park & Ride service, but with its fleet names covered over, Stagecoach Devon Alexander Dennis Trident 19569 (WA59 FWR) is seen at Eton Manor on Olympic duties on 1 August 2012.

With its identity covered over to meet the edict of the London Olympics committee, Stagecoach South Alexander Dennis Enviro300 27668 (GX10 KZW) is seen here near Tower Gateway, London, on 1 August 2012. (T. S. Blackman)

Although still displaying its route branding, Stagecoach Strathtay Alexander Dennis Trident 19655 (SP60 DPY), seen here leaving the Olympic bus park at Eton Manor on 1 August 2012, has had its owner's identity removed.

Stagecoach in the Twenty-First Century

Painted in Citylink joint venture livery with its identity hidden behind white vinyl panels, Stagecoach Highland Country Plaxton-bodied Volvo B12B 53112 is seen on Olympic duties at Eton Manor on 8 August 2012. (John Godwin)

Only the fleet names have been removed from Stagecoach Devon Alexander Dennis Trident 19325 (WA08 NPD), which retains its Go2 branding for the Exeter to Newton Abbot service, and is seen here on an Olympic shuttle service on 1 August 2012.

Waiting at the traffic lights near Eton Manor on 1 August 2010 while undertaking Olympic duties are Stagecoach South Alexander Dennis Enviro300 27644 (GX10 HBZ), in Coastliner 700 branded livery, and Stagecoach North West Alexander Dennis E40D 10029 (PX12 DNO), neither of which display fleet names.

Leaving Eton Manor Olympic bus park on 1 August 2012 are Stagecoach Midland Red Alexander Dennis E40D 10038 (KX12 GXG), which is totally devoid of any form of identification, and Stagecoach Eastbourne Alexander Dennis Enviro300 27579 (GX58 GKL), which has Uno route branding on its front panel.

Hired by Stagecoach from Ulsterbus for the duration of the London Olympics, Irizar-bodied Scania K114IB4 MCZ 6103, given temporary Stagecoach fleet number 80183 and megabus.com vinyls on its windscreen and above its front wheel arch, is seen here on a megabusplus duty at East Midlands Parkway railway station on 1 August 2012.

Stagecoach in the Twenty-First Century

Still in First livery, albeit with Stagecoach fleet names, Wright-bodied Volvo B7RLE 21244 (MX55 FGZ) and Wright-bodied Volvo B7TL 16959 (MX07 BVL) are seen in Wigan on 2 December 2102, after Stagecoach had taken over First's operations in the town. (K. S. E. Till)

A day after Stagecoach had taken over First Manchester's operations in Wigan, Optare Excel 35035 (R218 SBA), which was new to Timeline, is seen wearing its new fleet name and number on the 'Barbie' livery of its previous owner. (M. H. A. Flynn)

Seen at Wigan on 3 December 2012, having just been taken over from First Manchester by Stagecoach, East Lancs-bodied Dennis Arrow 13804 (R426 SOY) had begun life in London with Capital Citybus. (L. J. Long)

Also seen in Wigan after being taken over by Stagecoach from First Manchester is Irisbus Scolarbus 29817 (FX57 LKM), which is painted in a dedicated School Bus livery but has already gained a Stagecoach fleet name and number. (L. J. Long)

Alexander Dennis hybrid Enviro350H demonstrator SN62 DNJ is seen being evaluated at Chester on 12 February 2015 by Stagecoach, who has given it temporary fleet number 80023. (Author's collection)

Wright-bodied Volvo B7RLE demonstrator BK19 MGE is pictured in Liverpool on 15 January 2011 while being used by Stagecoach Merseyside, who had given it temporary fleet number 80013. (L. J. Long)

Standing outside the former First depot at Rock Ferry on 28 March 2013 after being taken over by Stagecoach is Alexander-bodied Volvo Olympian 16237 (S659 NUG), which began life with First Leeds. (L. J. Long)

Seen in Chester on 28 March 2013 after being repainted into Stagecoach corporate livery is Wright Eclipse Gemini-bodied Volvo B7TL 16964 (YJ04 FZE). New to First West Yorkshire, it had been acquired by Stagecoach with First's Wirral operations. (L. J. Long)

Painted in City Sightseeing Chester livery, and seen here on 26 March 2013, Stagecoach open-top ECW-bodied Leyland Olympian 14168 (D238 FYM) started life with London Buses as a conventional closed-top bus. (L. J. Long)

Seen on 8 September 2014, having been repainted into Stagecoach livery and used on a small number of school bus contracts taken over from First at Wrexham, Bluebird AARE 29880 (CX02 EGK) was originally operated by First PMT. (L. J. Long)

Stagecoach in the Twenty-First Century 77

About to leave Rock Ferry depot on 27 March 2013, Stagecoach Wright-bodied Scania L94UB 28531 (S102 TNB) still wears the 'Barbie' livery of its former owner. (L. J. Long)

Acquired with the business of Bluebird, Middleton, in whose livery it is seen here in Manchester on 4 March 2013, Alexander Dennis Enviro300 27600 (MX57 OEL) has gained its new owner's fleet name. (L. J. Long)

Purchased new by King's Lynn-based Norfolk Green, Alexander Dennis E40D 21 (SN12 EHM) was given fleet number 10052 when the company was taken over by Stagecoach. (T. S. Blackman)

Painted in SPT livery, Stagecoach West Scotland Alexander Dennis Enviro300 27597 (SN08 AEK) is seen here in Paisley while working a contract duty on 18 October 2013. (Murdoch Currie)

Being evaluated by Stagecoach Manchester, Alexander Dennis hybrid E40H demonstrator 80022 (SN63 VTX) is seen in Manchester Piccadilly bus station on 26 February 2014. (L. J. Long)

JMP of Middleton's East Lancs-bodied Volvo B7TL 534 (PN02 XBV), seen in Manchester on 29 March 2013, began life with Go-Ahead London Central. (M. H. A. Flynn)

Heading into Edinburgh on the 900 service from Glasgow, for which it is branded, is Stagecoach West Scotland Citylink joint venture-liveried Plaxton-bodied tri-axle Volvo B13RT 54132 (YX63 NGF). (Richard Walter)

Minus destination blinds, Stagecoach in Devon Northern Counties-bodied Volvo Olympian 16047 (M307 DGP) had been cascaded from Stagecoach Selkent, with whom it was operated as a dual-door bus. (B. Newsome)

Transferred to South Gloucestershire Bus & Coach Co. for continued use on megabus.com services is left-hand drive Van Hool Altano TX21 55013 (KX14 HSO). (South Gloucestershire Bus & Coach)

With megabus.com livery on its sides but a Stagecoach Oxford Tube front, Stagecoach Red & White Van Hool TD927 50237 (CN61 FAO) heads into London on 23 September 2018. (Richard Walter)

Stagecoach Selkent Wright-bodied Volvo B5LH 13012, seen here on 16 April 2018, displays an appropriate hybrid logo above its rear wheel arch. (L. J. Long)

Repainted into corporate livery and temporarily returned to service, Stagecoach Merseyside open-top ECW-bodied Leyland Olympian 14166 (D158 FYM) is seen here, lacking destination blinds, at New Brighton on 14 June 2014. (L. J. Long)

Operating a railway replacement service at Birkenhead on 29 September 2014 is Stagecoach Merseyside Alexander-bodied Dennis Trident 17575 (LV52 HFH), which retains the livery of Stagecoach Selkent, from whom it had been cascaded. (L. J. Long)

Having recently been converted to open-top configuration, and seen here operating Chester's city sightseeing tour on 29 September 2013, is Stagecoach Merseyside Alexander-bodied Dennis Trident 17502 (LX51 FNE), which had originally been a conventional closed-top bus with Stagecoach East London. (L. J. Long)

Wearing a dedicated livery for Chester Park & Ride is Stagecoach Merseyside Alexander Dennis E20D 20651 (SN16 OPF). (D. W. Rhodes)

Picking up its passengers in High Street, Irvine, on 24 August 2013 while operating route 23, for which it is branded, Stagecoach West Scotland Optare Solo 47836 (SF13 FNC) displays a 'town scene' between its headlights and a strap line to persuade motorists to 'leave the car at home'. (Murdoch Currie)

Parked outside Stagecoach Rennies Cowdenbeath depot on 19 January 2018 is Alexander-bodied Dennis Trident 17393 (Y393 NHK), which started life with Stagecoach East London in June 2001. (Richard Walter)

Jet branded for the 11A service to Inverness Airport is Stagecoach Highland Country Alexander-bodied Scania K230UB 28649 (SV12 AYK) seen here at Falcon Square, Inverness, on 31 March 2014. (Murdoch Currie)

Painted in a non-standard livery, Stagecoach East London LT271 (LTZ 1271), a Wright NBFL, is seen in the heart of the capital, heading along Holborn on 25 October 2014. (Nigel Eadon-Clarke)

Branded for route 73, and displaying logos relating to its electric hybrid credentials, Stagecoach Fife Alexander Dennis-bodied Volvo B5LH 13046 (SJ15 PVF) collects a healthy load of passengers – or are they customers? – in High Street, Dundee, on 15 June 2015. (Murdoch Currie)

Painted in White Lady livery to pay homage to Ribble's erstwhile double-deck coaches, Stagecoach North West open-top Alexander-bodied Dennis Trident 17012 (S812 BWC), which began life as a conventional bus with Stagecoach East London in January 1999, is pictured here operating the 505 tourist service in the Lake District. (Author's collection)

Seen at Peterborough in 2017 is Virgin Trains East Coast diesel-electric No. 43317, which was built by British Railways at Crewe Works in May 1979. (Author's collection)

Built for megabus.com's Anglo-Scottish sleeper coach services, and seen here at its launch at the O2 Arena in Greenwich, London, is Stagecoach West Scotland Van Hool TDX29 50301 (SF13 FMC), which, like its sisters, was later relegated to Citylink Gold services. (Stagecoach)

Wearing unconventional Express livery, Stagecoach Fife Plaxton Elite-bodied Volvo B11RT 54333 (YX66 WNT) is seen here in Edinburgh on 3 May 2018. (Richard Walter)

Promoting Stagecoach's Mega strategy, Alexander Dennis Enviro300 27531 (SP57 DFD) makes its way through Edinburgh on 28 July 2018. (Richard Walter)

Stagecoach Yorkshire Alexander Dennis E40D 10658 (YX66 WCZ), painted in a branded livery for the Townlines 66 service, is seen heading through Worsbrough Bridge in the Barnsley suburbs. (Stagecoach)

Wearing a promotional livery for Scotland's Charity Air Ambulance, Stagecoach East Scotland Plaxton Panther-bodied Volvo B13RT 54125 (SP62 CKF) heads into Edinburgh on 10 June 2018. (Richard Walter)

In memory of those killed and injured in the 2017 Manchester Arena attack, Stagecoach Manchester repainted Alexander Dennis Trident 19530 (MX09 KTO) in a commemorative livery to show support to the city. (Author's collection)

Following the demise of London's iconic Routemasters in 2005, TfL introduced two heritage services upon which Routemasters would continue to be operated. One, the 15 from Trafalgar Square to the Tower, was operated by Stagecoach East London, whose RM324 (WLT 324) is seen here on 9 December 2005. Painted in traditional London Transport livery, it carries its owner's name above its foremost lower deck side window.

Displaying Fastlink lettering, Stagecoach West Scotland Alexander Dennis E30D 27215 (SK15 HBP) is seen here at South Glasgow Hospital, ready to return to Glasgow city centre on the X1 service on 12 July 2015. (Murdoch Currie)

Stagecoach in the Twenty-First Century 91

Being evaluated by Stagecoach North East, all-electric Yutong TC12 demonstrator YK66 CBC is pictured at the Metro Centre, Gateshead, on 26 April 2018. (Stagecoach)

Caught by the camera at George Street, Chester, on 27 July 2018, gold-liveried Stagecoach Merseyside Optare Solo 47513 (TSV 779) started life with Stagecoach Midland Red, with whom it was registered KX57 KGK. (D. W. Rhodes)

Stagecoach Sunderland's gas-powered Alexander Dennis-bodied Scania K270UB 28029 (YR14 CGU) is seen here on 27 June 2018, having been freshly repainted into corporate livery. (Author's collection)

Having been converted to open-top format, Stagecoach East London Alexander-bodied Dennis Trident 18477 is seen here on 14 July 2018 while operating a megasightseeing.com tour in England's capital city. (Richard Walter)

Stagecoach in the Twenty-First Century 93

With Schoolrunner fleet names and painted in a new orange-red livery, Stagecoach North West Alexander-bodied Volvo Olympian 16640 (P270 VPN) is seen here in August 2018. (Author's collection)

Wearing Stagecoach Express livery, Stagecoach Fife Plaxton Panther-bodied tri-axle Volvo B8RLE 54506 (YX18 LHR) is seen leaving Buchanan bus station, Glasgow, on 22 May 2018.

Seen in a Stagecoach promotional photograph sporting a Matlock Bus fleet name is Stagecoach East Midlands Optare Solo 47063 (SF04 SKD), which was new to Stagecoach West Scotland. (Stagecoach)

Immaculately presented, and painted in Lakesider livery, is Stagecoach North West semi open-top Wright-bodied Volvo B5TL 13805 (BV17 CTU). (Author's collection)

Seen at London City Airport when new in July 2018 is Stagecoach East London Alexander Dennis E40D 11033 (SN18 KTX). (Stagecoach)

Branded for the X76 service from Kilmarnock and Glasgow is Stagecoach West Scotland Plaxton Elite-bodied Volvo B11RLE 50401 (YX18 LKK). It is seen here when new, in July 2018. (Stagecoach)

No. 399202 was one of the new Vossloh-built, dual-voltage Stagecoach Tram Trains employed on the service from Sheffield to Rotherham, which changes from light to heavy rail at Meadowhall. (Stagecoach)

Adorned in pre-Stagecoach Fife livery to celebrate 100 years of Dunfermline depot, Stagecoach Fife Alexander Dennis Enviro300 27532 (SV57 BYM) is pictured in Edinburgh on 21 September 2018. (Richard Walter)